CATECHETICAL FORMATION IN CHASTE LIVING

GUIDELINES FOR CURRICULUM DESIGN AND PUBLICATION

UNITED STATES CONFERENCE OF CATHOLIC BISHOPS
WASHINGTON, D.C.

The document *Catechetical Formation in Chaste Living: Guidelines for Curriculum Design and Publication* was developed by the Committee on Evangelization and Catechesis of the United States Conference of Catholic Bishops (USCCB). It was approved by the full body of the USCCB at its November 2007 General Meeting and has been authorized for publication by the undersigned.

Msgr. David J. Malloy, STD
General Secretary, USCCB

First printing, June 2008

ISBN: 978-1-60137-043-3

CONTENTS

INTRODUCTION

atechetical Formation in Chaste Living: Guidelines for Curriculum Design and Publication is designed to guide publishers in the development of new religion texts for students in preschool through twelfth grade and to assist in curriculum development by diocesan and parish catechetical leaders. These guidelines may also be helpful to assist parents/guardians, catechists, and Catholic school teachers in their respective roles in this crucial and delicate task.

The development of this document has been prompted by the promulgation of the teaching of the Church in the *Catechism of the Catholic Church* and by the publication of the *General Directory for Catechesis*, the *National Directory for Catechesis*, and the *United States Catholic Catechism for Adults*. This new set of catechetical guidelines focuses specifically on catechetical formation in Catholic faith and morals as well as on virtues for chaste living. Proper reference to human anatomy or physiology is to be made only to the degree necessary to teach morality and virtue. The content of these guidelines acknowledges the primary role of parents in giving a concrete or more specific education in human sexuality. The teaching of the *Catechism of the Catholic Church*, the *General Directory for Catechesis*, and the *National Directory for Catechesis* is normative in this area, and consultation of these documents is presumed by these guidelines.

All of catechesis on chaste living takes place within the faith community that is the Church. Everyone involved in this catechesis is only able to instruct because each has first received the teaching of the Church. Parents are particularly responsible for catechizing their children in faith and morals and thus have a special obligation to understand thoroughly and live the teachings of the Church. Assisting parents of adolescents and youth in the formation of their children for chaste living is essential to their formation in the Catholic faith and should be mandatory in Catholic schools and in parish religious education and youth ministry programs. This may be done in the form of a curriculum, a presentation for youth and/or parents, or the use of other educational materials.

Through the implementation of these guidelines, it is hoped that each baptized person becomes able to

a. Reflect upon and cherish his or her dignity and that of other persons as made in the image and likeness of God
b. Reflect faithfully that image in a life conformed to new life in Christ
c. Deepen the relationship with Christ and the Church through frequent prayer and celebration of the sacraments, especially the Sacrament of Penance and Reconciliation and the Sacrament of the Eucharist

d. Embrace joyfully the call to love and live chastely either as a married person or as a celibate person

Jesus Christ has won salvation for all through his saving life, Death, Resurrection, and Ascension. In Baptism, with the forgiveness of Original Sin and the gift of baptismal grace, the Lord helps people to grow in holiness and virtue; to live as his adopted children and as members of his Body, the Church; and to love each other as he has loved us. Guided by the Holy Spirit and the relationship of love within the Holy Trinity which has been given to the entire world, Christ's disciples are called to live in relationships which demonstrate this same love of God.

Faithful to the Lord Jesus Christ's life and teaching, the Church continues to proclaim salvation in Christ Jesus and to invite men and women to follow his way. Though humanity is still wounded by sin, the Church continues to call all to trust in God's mercy, to turn away from sin, and to embrace the Good News. She continues to teach everyone how to live as Jesus did, instructing them in the message of the Ten Commandments, the Beatitudes, and the entire Gospel. She urges frequent reception of the sacraments, especially Penance and Reconciliation and the Eucharist, and cultivation of the virtues that enable people to lead a chaste and holy life.

PART I:
THE TEACHING OF THE CHURCH

A. *The Received Teaching of the Church Regarding Chaste Living*

Catechetical instruction in chaste living needs to treat doctrinal truths insofar as they apply to the integration of the human mind, heart, will, and body. Catechetical instruction should include the following components.

RECEIVED TEACHING OF THE CHURCH	REFERENCES
1. Human beings are created in God's own image and created for love: to receive God's love in order to love God, ourselves, and our neighbor; and to receive love from others. To love is to will the good of another.	Gn 1:26-27 CCC, nos. 1604, 2093, 2105, 1766 *Familiaris Consortio*, no. 11
2. Individually, as male or female, human beings reflect creation in the image and likeness of God by having an intellect, a free will, and the capacity of free truly human and moral acts. A person's gender is also constitutive of his or her nature and spirituality.	Gn 1:27 CCC, nos. 355, 1700, 1704-1706 *Veritatis Splendor*, nos. 35, 40 *Theology of the Body*, 37, 42, 52-53, 61
3. Being created in God's image also enables human beings to share in Trinitarian love, and to express love in marriage through the generation of new life and through self-donation. This call to communion is revealed in the complementarity of the bodies of men and women, which are capable of becoming "one flesh" and expressing the mutual gift of self that marriage ought to be.	*Gaudium et Spes*, no. 49 CCC, nos. 27, 371-372, 2331-2334 *Truth and Meaning*, no. 10 *Theology of the Body*, 45, 47

4. Adam and Eve shared in God's friendship (grace) but lost it through a free act of disobedience called Original Sin. "Although set by God in a state of rectitude, man, enticed by the evil one, abused his freedom at the very start of history. He lifted himself up against God and sought to attain his goal apart from him." By his sin, Adam, as the first man, lost the original holiness and justice he had received from God, not only for himself but for all human beings. Adam and Eve transmitted to their descendants a human nature wounded by their own first sin and hence deprived of original holiness and justice; this deprivation is called "Original Sin."

Rom 5:12-14
Gaudium et Spes, no. 13
CCC, nos. 397, 415-417, 1707

5. The effects of Original Sin include
  • Loss of God's friendship (grace)
  • Damage to the harmony between body, intellect, and will
  • Reduced ability to love one another unselfishly
  • Experience of shame
  • Confusion about the nature and purpose of the human body
  • Being subject to other temptations to sin and to concupiscence
  • Death

CCC, nos. 399-400, 418
CCC, no. 1707
Gn 3:7-11

Rom 1:18-32

Truth and Meaning, no. 11
CCC, nos. 1707, 1869, 1008

CCC, nos. 1264, 1426

CCC, no. 1008

6. God did not abandon his people. From the moment the first humans committed Original Sin, God revealed his plan for everyone's redemption.

CCC, nos. 55, 410-411

7. To accomplish our redemption, God the Father sent his Son, Jesus Christ, true God and true man, to give us the Holy Spirit.

CCC, no. 461

8. Jesus Christ knows and loves us, and by his suffering and death, he gives himself up for each one of us and brings about our redemption within the community of the Church.

CCC, nos. 604-605, 1708

9. Not only did Jesus Christ, the Son of God, redeem us, he also taught us how to live and gave us the gift of new life through the power of the Holy Spirit.

CCC, no. 1709
Veritatis Splendor, nos. 15-18

10. Christian morality consists in following Christ, being transformed by his grace and renewed in his mercy.

CCC, nos. 424-428
Veritatis Splendor, nos. 19-24

11. Moral formation involves a journey of interior transformation that deepens one's personal conversion to Christ.

CCC, no. 1709
Veritatis Splendor, no. 25

12. We do not lead the moral life on our own. God helps and transforms us from within by the power of his grace. In freedom, we are called to cooperate with God's grace.

CCC, nos. 1742, 2001, 2022

13. A virtue is a habitual and firm disposition to do what is right and good.

CCC, no. 1803

14. The *cardinal virtues* of prudence, justice, fortitude, and temperance play a pivotal role in governing our actions, ordering our passions, and guiding our conduct according to reason and faith. These virtues are acquired by human efforts as a result of education, by deliberate acts, and by perseverance ever renewed in repeated morally good acts. All human virtues are related to the cardinal virtues, and all are purified and elevated by divine grace.

CCC, nos. 1805, 1810

15. The *theological virtues* of faith, hope, and
love (charity) are the foundation of Christian
moral activity. They animate it and give it its
special character. They aid persons to grow in a
generous and self-giving love that is the foundation for a chaste life.

CCC, nos. 1812, 1813

16. The *seven gifts of the Holy Spirit* are wisdom,
understanding, counsel, fortitude, knowledge,
piety, and fear of the Lord. They complete and
perfect the virtues of those who receive them.

CCC, no. 1831

17. It is not easy for man, wounded by sin, to
maintain moral balance. Christ's gift of salvation
offers us the grace necessary to persevere in the
pursuit of the virtues. Everybody should also ask
for this grace of light and strength, frequent the
sacraments, cooperate with the Holy Spirit, and
follow his call to seek what is good and avoid
evil. If we are united with the Lord, we will
reach fulfillment in the glory of heaven.

CCC, nos. 1709, 1715, 1811

18. This glory is experienced in part through
the *twelve fruits of the Holy Spirit* at work in us:
charity, joy, peace, patience, kindness, goodness,
generosity, gentleness, faithfulness, modesty,
self-control, chastity.

CCC, no. 1832

19. The Ten Commandments, the Beatitudes,
and the Four Precepts of the Church instruct
us in how we are to live our lives in union
with God.

Ex 20:2-17

Dt 5:6-21

Mt 5:3-12

CCC, nos. 1716, 1717, 1724,
1952, 2041, 2072

Veritatis Splendor, no. 16

20. Chastity is a virtue that allows us to do what
is right, good, and truly loving in the areas of
relationship and sexuality. All the baptized are
called to cultivate this spiritual power which
frees love from selfishness and aggression. The
virtue of chastity shines out with incomparable
splendor in the virginity of Jesus Christ.

CCC, no. 2348
Truth and Meaning, no. 16
Mt 19:1-12; Rom 5:12ff.; 1 Cor
    15:45-47; Col 1:1-18

CCC, nos. 2345, 359, 504-05, 518
Sacramentum Caritatis, no. 24

21. Chastity promotes the full integration of
sexuality within persons, in accord with their
state of life—married, single, professed religious,
or consecrated celibate. Chastity promotes
abstention from immoral sexual activity.

CCC, nos. 2337, 2349

22. Chastity includes an apprenticeship in self-
mastery, which is a training in human freedom
and which is the result of long and hard
personal and interior work.

CCC, nos. 2339, 2342

23. Chastity flows from the moral virtue of temperance that helps us direct our sexuality and
sexual desires toward authentic love and away
from using persons as objects for sexual plea-
sure. Chastity is not a matter of repression of
sexual feelings and temptations but is the suc-
cessful integration of the gift of sexuality within
the whole person. To integrate the gift of sexuality means to make it subordinate to love and
respect through the practice of chastity.

CCC, no. 2341
Truth and Meaning, no. 4

24. Formation in the virtue of chastity includes   CCC, nos. 2338-2345, 2517-2527
- Education for authentic love   NDC, §45 °F
- Understanding of one's sexuality as a gift   *Truth and Meaning*, nos. 8-25
- Cultivation of all the virtues, especially charity
- The practice of prayer
- The virtue of temperance
- Respect for human dignity in oneself and in others
- The practice of decency and modesty in behavior, dress, and speech
- Respect for one's own body and for others as temples of the Holy Spirit   1 Cor 6:19
- Assistance in acquiring self-mastery and self-control

25. The benefits of chastity include   CCC, nos. 2338-2340
- The integrity of life and love placed in the person   CCC, no. 2338
- The gift of authentic friendship   CCC, no. 2347
- Fidelity in marriage, which leads to strong family life   CCC, no. 2363
- The ability to be "pure of heart"   CCC, no. 2518
- Development to authentic maturity   *Familiaris Consortio*, no. 37
- Capacity to respect and foster the "nuptial meaning" of the body   *Familiaris Consortio*, no. 37
- A lifestyle that brings joy   *Truth and Meaning*, no. 3
- The discipline to renounce self, make sacrifices, and wait   *Truth and Meaning*, no. 5
- A life that revolves around self-giving love   *Truth and Meaning*, no. 16
- Development of a harmonious personality   *Truth and Meaning*, no. 17
- Freedom from all forms of self-centeredness   *Truth and Meaning*, no. 17
- The capacity for compassion, tolerance, generosity, and a spirit of sacrifice   *Truth and Meaning*, no. 31
- Avoidance of occasions of sin

26. Christ's disciples need to be aware of and to resist temptation to engage in activities which are violations of chastity with varying degrees of gravity, such as

- Immodest behavior, dress, or speech
- Misuse of the Internet creating easy access to virtual and anonymous behaviors for viewing pornography, for being preyed upon by others, for writing explicitly through blogs and instant messaging, and for posting inappropriate, sexually explicit, or suggestive photos, messages, rumors, etc. on popular social networking Web sites
- Risky behaviors, sometimes as a result of using alcohol and drugs, which often lead to sexual encounters
- Giving in to lustful desires and temptations
- Viewing pornography and indecent entertainment
- Masturbation
- Use of contraceptives
- Use of illicit reproductive technologies
- All forms of premarital sex, including oral sex
- Cohabitation
- Homosexual sexual activity
- Adultery
- Polygamy
- Prostitution
- Rape
- Incest
- Sexual abuse

Mt 5:27-28
Rom 8:5-10, 12-13
Eph 5:3-7

Gal 5:13, 17-21; 6:7-10
CCC, nos. 2351-2359, 2380-2381, 2389, 2400

NDC, §45 °F
Veritatis Splendor, no. 26

27. Violations of chastity are sinful, some
of them gravely sinful. To die in mortal sin
without repenting and accepting God's merciful
love means remaining separated from him
forever. Mortal sins against chastity bring great
risk to our salvation and open the possibility
for eternal damnation.

CCC, nos. 1033, 2352

28. For any who fail to live chaste lives, Jesus
Christ offers through his Church opportunities for forgiveness through the Sacrament of
Penance and Reconciliation. Regular reception
of the Sacrament of the Eucharist, as well as
prayer and good works, can help us maintain
chaste living. We need God's grace to help us
live a chaste life.

*CCC, nos. 1391-1395, 1426,
1434-1437, 1446, 1468-1469,
1484, 2337-2345*

29. Conjugal love between husband and wife is
part of God's plan for humanity. Marriage is a
lifelong communion of a man and woman con-
stituted by a mutual gift of self which is called to
image the inner life of the Trinity. When conjugal love is faithful, exclusive, and open to life, it
is a blessing to the couple and, through them, to
the Church and to the world.

*Mt 19; Mt 5:27-30
CCC, nos. 2360-2379
Gaudium et Spes, nos. 48-52*

30. Married people are called to love in conjugal
chastity, while those unmarried live a chastity
of continence.

CCC, no. 2349

31. In the battle for purity and purification of
the heart, the Blessed Virgin Mary will assist
persons to live a chaste life.

*CCC, nos. 2514-2533
Truth and Meaning, no. 71*

B. Church Teaching on Special Issues of Concern

Serious concerns are identified because of their prevalence in our society today and the particular dangers they pose to chaste living. In dealing with these special issues, the teaching of the Church must be presented with clarity. It should also be clear that for those who are affected by these and other similar issues, the Church responds with pastoral compassion, reaching out to support and encourage all who struggle to live moral lives.

TOPIC	REFERENCES
1. Pornography Any efforts to portray real or simulated sexual acts in order to display them to others uses persons as objects and betrays the meaning of sexuality. Pornography defames the intimacy of the marital act and injures the dignity of viewers and participants. Child pornography is a particularly abhorrent form of pornography that dehumanizes children for profit or perverted pleasure. Christians are to shun all participation in pornography as producers, actors, consumers, or vendors. Pornography also tends to become addictive. The ready availability of pornography on the Internet and television adds to the spread of this addiction.	CCC, no. 2354

2. Contraceptive Mentality and Practice

In the marital act, the unity of the spouses
and the gift of life go together. Both are good
as created by God for couples. Contraception,
which separates openness to life from the act of
conjugal unity in sexual intercourse, has become
such a commonly accepted practice that many
choose to engage in it without any reference to
the moral aspect of their actions. Contraception
is contrary to the law of God. Pope Paul VI, in
Humanae Vitae, prophetically identified conse-
quences that would come about as a result of
an acceptance of contraception. These include
marital infidelity, a lessening of moral standards,
a loss of respect for women and their dignity,
governments limiting the number of births
allowed, less personal responsibility toward
others, more selfish individualism, harm to the
family, and growth in a materialistic approach to
life. Some commonly accepted types of contraception are abortifacients.

CCC, no. 2370
Humanae Vitae, nos. 8, 17
Familiaris Consortio, nos. 89-90

3. Premarital and Extramarital Sex

Acts proper and exclusive to spouses are totally
reserved for a man and a woman who are joined
in marriage and committed to one another
until death. All other carnal unions and sexual
acts (including oral sex) between an unmarried man and woman (fornication), or between
two partners of whom at least one is married
to another party (adultery), violate the Sixth
Commandment and are serious offenses against
chastity and/or the dignity of marriage. Married
couples have always experienced problems that
threaten their union: jealousy, infidelity, and
conflicts. Lust and arbitrary domination can
ruin a marriage. These situations can lead to
mental, physical, and emotional abuse.

CCC, nos. 1643-1648, 2348-2350,
2360-2361, 2380, 2394

*United States Catholic Catechism for
Adults*, 287-288

4. Divorce

When a marriage has broken down, there is a presumption of validity until the contrary is proven. The Church tribunal provides a process whereby an examination of the marriage can be made and possible invalidity determined. When faced with separation and divorce, Catholics should be encouraged and supported to make every effort to seek reconciliation. If even this fails, they should be assisted in seeking the services of the tribunal, if they so choose. In today's culture, the Church's fidelity to Christ's teaching on marriage and against divorce should remain strong. Great sensitivity and pastoral care should be offered to those Catholics who have experienced the pain of civil divorce but who wish to keep the faith and who desire to bring up their children in the Catholic faith, so they do not consider themselves alienated from the Catholic faith.

Canon 1676

5. Cohabitation

"Cohabitation" is a term used to describe the living arrangement of sexually active couples who are not married but are living as husband and wife. Cohabitation does not support the good of spouses, since the marriage union does not exist. It also does not provide a stable, permanent relationship for children who may be conceived. Cohabitation implies immoral sexual activity and, therefore, scandal. Whatever the reason that may be advanced, cohabitation is not a moral or acceptable preparation for marriage. In fact, cohabitation has been demonstrated to have a negative effect on the ultimate success of a marriage.

CCC, nos. 2350, 2353, 2390-2391

Familiaris Consortio, no. 81

*Family, Marriage, and
  "De Facto" Unions*

6. Sexual Abuse

Any sexual abuse perpetrated by an adult on
children, young people, or other vulnerable
individuals causes grave harm to the victim's
physical, psychological/emotional, and moral
integrity. Such actions are grave violations of
God's law. They are also criminal acts. Any
occurrence of sexual abuse of minors must be
reported to the proper civil authorities according to the *Charter for the Protection of Children
and Young People* as implemented in each dio-
cese. Further, reporting of abuse or suspected
abuse must be done in adherence with local
law. Likewise, the enslavement or trafficking of
humans, especially children, to force them into
prostitution or pornography; sexual abuse of
adults; and marital rape are also heinous forms
of sexual abuse. In addition, children need to
be instructed, in age-appropriate ways, that they
must never keep secret inappropriate actions
by adults.

CCC, nos. 2388-2389

7. Homosexual Activity

Although the existence of homosexual tenden-
cies is not sinful, divine and natural law teaches
that homosexual acts are gravely contrary to
chastity, intrinsically disordered, contrary to
the natural law, and closed to the gift of life;
they do not proceed from a genuine affective
and sexual complementarity and can never be
approved. Nonetheless, in her pastoral care, the
Church teaches that every person be treated
with respect, compassion, and sensitivity regard-
less of sexual orientation.

CCC, nos. 2357-2359, 2396
*Ministry to Persons with a
Homosexual Inclination*

8. Same-Sex "Marriage"

This phrase is used to describe a union between individuals of the same sex which mimics marriage. Whether or not sanctioned by the state, so-called same-sex "unions" or "marriages" do not contain the elements essential to God's plan for marriage. They lack the benefit of a nuptial or sacramental covenant and the ability to generate new human life. Because they are contrary to divine law and natural law, same-sex "unions" or "marriages" are intrinsically wrong and sinful.

CCC, nos. 1617, 1625, 1638-1640, 1643, 1652, 1659-1660, 1664

9. Reproductive Technology

Science and technology play an increasing role in our lives. What is learned and developed must always be at the service of the human person in accord with God's law. The desire to have a child is a natural one, but not one that can be fulfilled by any means whatever. A child is a gift from God and should be conceived through a conjugal act of love between parents. Conception must never be separated in any way or form from the conjugal act. All forms of *in vitro* fertilization, efforts at cloning a human person, and embryonic stem cell research are sinful.

CCC, nos. 2376-2377
Donum Vitae, §II °B, 4

PART II:
PASSING ON THE TEACHING
OF THE CHURCH

A. *The Role of Pastors*

TEACHING	REFERENCES
1. The Church has both a duty and a right to ensure that all the faithful are adequately educated and formed in the Catholic faith, particularly in the areas of chaste living and the Gospel of life.	Canons 794-795 *Veritatis Splendor*, nos. 27-28, 30
2. The pastors of the Church, under the direction of and in communion with their bishop, have a responsibility to serve as models of chaste living for the community as they work to ensure that the education and formation of all the faithful in chaste living is in accord with the Church's teaching.	Canon 773
3. This formation includes catechesis on the nature and vocation of men and women created in the image of God and called to form bonds of loving and chaste communion with one another through friendship, service, single life, marriage, and celibacy for the sake of the Kingdom.	*Gaudium et Spes*, nos. 49-52 Canon 777 §§3-5 *Truth and Meaning*, nos. 26-36

4. Some of the serious duties of a pastor include providing for catechesis of the Christian faithful; instructing and assisting parents/guardians on their role as primary educators of their children in the ways of the faith consistent with Church teaching; providing formation of those who catechize others—including parents/guardians involved in the catechesis of their children—in the area of chaste living; and providing ample opportunities for the Sacrament of Penance and Reconciliation.

Canons 528 §1, 773, 776
NDC, §54 °B, 1-2

5. The Church holds that it is her duty to instill confidence in parents about their own capabilities and to help them carry out their task.

Truth and Meaning, no. 47

6. Under the direction of the pastor, Catholic schools, religious education programs, and youth ministry programs should provide assistance as catechetical partners with parents or guardians. Formation in chaste living is an integral part of the Church's instruction in the moral life and becomes part of the overall catechetical curriculum. Teachers and catechists should be adequately formed in chaste living, so as to reinforce and support the teachings to be handled by parents/guardians.

Canons 796, 798, 1063 §4
Familiaris Consortio, no. 14
NDC, §54 °B, 1-2

B. *The Role of Parents/Guardians*

TEACHING	REFERENCES
1. Marriage is designed by the Creator to promote the good of the spouses and to provide for the procreation and education of children.	*Gaudium et Spes*, no. 48 CCC, nos. 2366-2367 Canon 1055 §1 *Truth and Meaning*, no. 15
2. Parents/guardians are to be the first and foremost educators of their children. This God-given responsibility cannot legitimately be taken away by other powers or institutions.	CCC, no. 2221 *Gravissimum Educationis*, no. 3 Canons 774 §2, 1136 *Familiaris Consortio*, no. 36 NDC, §54 °C; §61 °A, 3
3. Parents/guardians are called to practice and witness marital chastity and to build a very positive relationship between themselves that strengthens their marital covenant and guards against the perils of divorce.	CCC, nos. 2349, 2363-2365 Canon 1063 §4 *Familiaris Consortio*, nos. 33-34 NDC, §36 °C, 2
4. Parents/guardians are obliged to ensure that their children's education in human sexuality occurs within the context of the moral principles and truths of the Catholic Church, whether it be done at home or in educational centers chosen by them.	Canons 226 §2, 835 §4 *Familiaris Consortio*, no. 37 *Truth and Meaning*, nos. 37-47

5. Education of children includes formation in knowledge and practice of their faith, including participation in Sunday Mass and frequent confession, a life of virtue in accordance with the teachings of the Church, catechesis on morality including education in chastity and the virtues, and the fostering of a growing relationship with Jesus according to the child's age and maturity level and in conformity with the teachings of the Catholic Church. Baptismal sponsors are also bound to provide support in this responsibility.

Canons 226, 774 §2, 914
CCC, nos. 2221-2226, 2229
NDC, §45 °F
Truth and Meaning, nos. 65-76

6. Christian parents/guardians are the primary but not the exclusive educators of their children. They carry out their role in communion with the Church and her pastors, who have a responsibility to ensure that the education offered to the young is in accordance with Church teaching.

Familiaris Consortio, nos. 36, 40
Truth and Meaning, nos. 20, 22

7. Parents/guardians are assisted by their pastors, from the spiritual riches of the Church, to receive ongoing Christian formation and to choose the means and institutes which can best promote the Catholic education of their children.

Canons 213, 217, 529 §1, 776, 793, 851 §2, 1063 §1
CCC, no. 2229
Familiaris Consortio, no. 37

8. The invitation to other educators to carry out their responsibilities in the name of the parents arises from the consent and authorization of the parents.

CCC, no. 2229

9. Parents are encouraged to review the *Catechism of the Catholic Church, The Truth and Meaning of Human Sexuality: Guidelines for Education Within the Family*, and the *National Directory for Catechesis* in fulfilling their roles.

CCC, nos. 1691-1876, 1949-2051, 2331-2400, 2514-2533
NDC, §45, §54 °C
Truth and Meaning

C. *The Role of Teachers and Catechists*

TEACHING	REFERENCES

1. *Content of Instruction*

Catechetical formation in chaste living must be presented according to the doctrinal and moral teaching of the Church.

CCC, nos. 1691-1876, 1949-2051, 2331-2400, 2514-2533

- Catholic educators should also consult the *National Directory for Catechesis* for a detailed listing of pertinent catechetical guidelines under general moral catechesis and under catechesis for the Sixth and Ninth Commandments.

  NDC, §§40-42, §45 °F

- Further guidelines are detailed in *The Truth and Meaning of Human Sexuality*.

  Truth and Meaning

- Teachers and catechists are obliged to use only those textbooks which have received the requisite ecclesiastical approval.

  NDC, §68 °A

- Catechists should be living witnesses of all virtue, since such witness is an essential part of catechesis.

2. Relationship of Educators to Parents

The Church teaches:

- "No one is capable of giving moral education regarding responsible personal growth in human sexuality better than duly prepared parents."

  Familiaris Consortio, no. 37

- Since the Church recognizes that parents are the first educators of their children, Catholic educators do well to focus on providing assistance to parents/guardians. Suitable materials need to be developed and provided to assist parents in their important responsibility.

  Truth and Meaning, no. 145

- Education for chastity, sustained by parental example and prayer, is absolutely essential to develop authentic maturity, teach respect for the body, and foster an understanding of the dignity of the body as the temple of the Holy Spirit and an understanding of the nuptial meaning of the body.

  Theology of the Body, 63
  CCC, no. 364

- Catechists must teach by their example and must love their students, so as to create a love for the truth in those that they teach.

  NDC, §55 °B
  Evangelii Nuntiandi, no. 41

3. Catechetical Process

- Catechetical formation in chaste living
  is best taught in stages according to each
  child's age and maturity.

  Truth and Meaning, nos. 52-63, 118-120, 123

- Education for chastity is more than a call
  to abstinence. It requires

  NDC, §48

  a. Understanding the need for a
     family environment of love, virtue,
     and respect for the gifts of God
  b. Learning the practice of decency,
     modesty, and self-control
  c. Guiding sexual instincts toward loving
     service of others

     CCC, no. 2339

  d. Recognizing one's embodied existence
     as male or female as a gift from God
  e. Discerning one's vocation to marriage,
     to chaste single life, to celibate priest-
     hood, or to consecrated virginity for
     the sake of the Kingdom of Heaven

     CCC, no. 2349

D. *The Role of Publishers*

TEACHING	REFERENCES
1. To the publishers and authors falls the crucial role of translating these doctrinal principles into texts and other materials for use with multiple audiences, including parents, families, schools, and religious education and youth ministry programs, in an age-appropriate manner.	
2. Catechetical formation in chaste living must be presented according to the doctrinal and moral teaching of the Catholic Church as outlined in these guidelines.	NDC, §70 °A (bullet 4, item 7) *Donum Vitae*, §III, nos. 14-15
3. Publishers should present the teaching of the Church regarding chaste living as a positive way to respond to encounters with Christ, who transforms our lives.	
4. To guide publishers and authors in their work, appropriate references from many sources, including the *Catechism of the Catholic Church*, Pope John Paul II's *Theology of the Body*, *The Truth and Meaning of Human Sexuality*, the *National Directory for Catechesis*, and the *United States Catholic Catechism for Adults* have been cited.	
5. In particular, publishers are directed to see the *National Directory for Catechesis* for a detailed listing of pertinent catechetical guidelines under general moral catechesis and under catechesis for the Sixth and Ninth Commandments.	NDC, §§40-42, §45 °F

6. Publishers are also directed to utilize the eight elements of human methodology as appropriate in developing formation resources for chaste living.

NDC, §29

7. Preparation of catechetical materials should also be based on sound principles of catechetical methodology that reflect the diversity of age, maturity, culture, race, ethnicity, and ecclesial conditions of those who will use the materials.

Canon 779
NDC, §70 °A, 6

8. Publishers are directed to honor the family, especially the role of parents as primary educators, when developing texts and other materials.

Familiaris Consortio, nos. 36-41

9. In late adolescence, young people can first be introduced to the knowledge of the signs of fertility and then to the natural regulation of fertility, but only in the context of education for love, fidelity in marriage, God's plan for procreation, and respect for human life.

Familiaris Consortio, no. 33
Truth and Meaning, no. 125
NDC, §36 °C, 2

10. Homosexuality should be discussed at an appropriate age and time and in an appropriate manner that respects people of all sexual inclination. When treated, it must be treated in terms of chaste living, an understanding of human sexuality, and the need for pastoral care for the person and the family.

Truth and Meaning, no. 125
Ministry to Persons with a Homosexual Inclination

E. *Resources*

Scripture

New American Bible.

Conciliar Decrees

Second Vatican Council. *Declaration on Christian Education* (*Gravissimum Educationis*), October 28, 1965.

Second Vatican Council. *Pastoral Constitution on the Church in the Modern World* (*Gaudium et Spes*), December 7, 1965.

Canon Law

Code of Canon Law: Latin-English Edition: New English Translation (*Codex Iuris Canonici* [CIC]). Washington, DC: Canon Law Society of America, 1998.

Documents of the Universal Church

Catechism of the Catholic Church (2nd ed.). Libreria Editrice Vaticana–United States Conference of Catholic Bishops, 2000.

Compendium of the Catechism of the Catholic Church. Libreria Editrice Vaticana–United States Conference of Catholic Bishops, 2006.

Papal Documents (Chronological)

Pius XI. Encyclical Letter *On Christian Marriage* (*Casti Connubii*), December 31, 1930.

Paul VI. Encyclical Letter *On the Regulation of Birth* (*Humanae Vitae*), July 25, 1968.

Paul VI. Apostolic Exhortation *On Evangelization in the Modern World* (*Evangelii Nuntiandi*), December 8, 1975.

John Paul II. Post-Synodal Apostolic Exhortation *The Role of the Christian Family in the Modern World* (*Familiaris Consortio*), November 22, 1981.

John Paul II. Encyclical Letter *The Splendor of Truth* (*Veritatis Splendor*), August 6, 1993.

John Paul II. *The Theology of the Body: Human Love in the Divine Plan.* Boston: Pauline Books & Media, 1997.

Benedict XVI. Post-Synodal Apostolic Exhortation *The Sacrament of Charity* (*Sacramentum Caritatis*), February 22, 2007.

Documents from Vatican Offices or Congregations

Congregation for Catholic Education. *Educational Guidance in Human Love,* 1983. Available at *www.vatican.va.*

Congregation for the Clergy. *General Directory for Catechesis.* Washington, DC: United States Conference of Catholic Bishops, 1997.

Congregation for the Doctrine of the Faith. *Instruction on Respect for Human Life in Its Origin and on the Dignity of Procreation: Replies to Certain Questions of the Day* (*Donum Vitae*), February 22, 1987. Available at *www.vatican.va.*

Congregation for the Doctrine of the Faith. *On Some Aspects of the Use of the Instruments of Social Communication in Promoting the Doctrine of the Faith,* March 30, 1992. Available at *www.vatican.va.*

Pontifical Council for the Family. *Family, Marriage, and "De Facto" Unions.* Washington, DC: United States Conference of Catholic Bishops, 2001.

Pontifical Council for the Family. *The Truth and Meaning of Human Sexuality: Guidelines for Education Within the Family.* Washington, DC: United States Conference of Catholic Bishops, 1996.

Documents from the USCCB

Ministry to Persons with a Homosexual Inclination: Guidelines for Pastoral Care. Washington, DC: United States Conference of Catholic Bishops, 2006.

National Directory for Catechesis. Washington, DC: United States Conference of Catholic Bishops, 2005.

Renewing the Vision: A Framework for Catholic Youth Ministry. Washington, DC: United States Conference of Catholic Bishops, 1997.

United States Catholic Catechism for Adults. Washington, DC: United States Conference of Catholic Bishops, 2006.